Nutrition for Achievement in Sports and Academics

Mason Crest
450 Parkway Drive, Suite D
Broomall, PA 19008
www.masoncrest.com

Printed and bound in the United States of America.

First printing
9 8 7 6 5 4 3 2 1

Series ISBN: 978-1-4222-2874-6
Hardcover ISBN: 978-1-4222-2884-5
ebook ISBN: 978-1-4222-8946-4
Paperback ISBN: 978-1-4222-2990-3

The Library of Congress has cataloged the
            hardcopy format(s) as follows:

Library of Congress Cataloging-in-Publication Data

Crockett, Kyle A.
   Nutrition for achievement in sports and academics / Kyle A. Crockett.
       pages cm. – (Understanding nutrition : a gateway to physical & mental health)
   Audience: Grade 4 to 6.
   ISBN 978-1-4222-2884-5 (hardcover) – ISBN 978-1-4222-2874-6 (series) – ISBN 978-1-4222-2990-3 (paperback) –ISBN 978-1-4222-8946-4 (ebook)
   1. Children–Nutrition–Juvenile literature. 2. Students–Nutrition–Juvenile literature. 3. Athletes–Nutrition–Juvenile literature. 4. Physical fitness–Nutritional aspects–Juvenile literature. 5. Success–Juvenile literature. 6. Health–Juvenile literature. I. Title.
   TX355.C83 2014
   641.5'622–dc23
                                            2013009807

Produced by Vestal Creative Services.
www.vestalcreative.com

UNDERSTANDING NUTRITION:
A GATEWAY TO PHYSICAL AND MENTAL HEALTH

Nutrition for Achievement in Sports and Academics

KYLE A. CROCKETT

Mason Crest

CONTENTS

INTRODUCTION
by Dr. Joshua Borus

There are many decisions to make about food. Almost everyone wants to "eat healthy"—but what does that really mean? What is the "right" amount of food and what is a "normal" portion size? Do I need sports drinks if I'm an athlete—or is water okay? Are all "organic" foods healthy? Getting reliable information about nutrition can be confusing. All sorts of restaurants and food makers spend billions of dollars trying to get you to buy their products, often by implying that a food is "good for you" or "healthy." Food packaging has unbiased, standardized nutrition labels, but if you don't know what to look for, they can be hard to understand. Magazine articles and the Internet seem to always have information about the latest fad diets or new "superfoods" but little information you can trust. Finally, everyone's parents, friends, and family have their own views on what is healthy. How are you supposed to make good decisions with all this information when you don't know how to interpret it?

The goal of this series is to arm you with information to help separate what is healthy from not healthy. The books in the series will help you think about things like proper portion size and how eating well can help you stay healthy, improve your mood, and manage your weight. These books will also help you take action. They will let you know some of the changes you can make to keep healthy and how to compare eating options.

Keep in mind a few broad rules:

- First, healthy eating is a lifelong process. Learning to try new foods, preparing foods in healthy ways, and focusing on the big picture are essential parts of that process. Almost no one can keep on a very restrictive diet for a long time or entirely cut out certain groups of foods, so it's best to figure out how to eat healthy in a way that's realistic for you by making a number of small changes.

- Second, a lot of healthy eating hasn't really changed much over the years and isn't that complicated once you know what to look for. The core of a healthy diet is still eating reasonable portions at regular meals. This should be mostly fruits and vegetables, reasonable amounts of proteins, and lots of whole grains, with few fried foods or extra fats. "Junk food" and sweets also have their place—they taste good and have a role in celebrations and other happy events—but they aren't meant to be a cornerstone of your diet!

- Third, avoid drinks with calories in them, beverages like sodas, iced tea, and most juices. Try to make your liquid intake all water and you'll be better off.

- Fourth, eating shouldn't be done mindlessly. Often people will munch while they watch TV or play games because it's something to do or because they're bored rather then because they are hungry. This can lead to lots of extra food intake, which usually isn't healthy. If you are eating, pay attention, so that you are enjoying what you eat and aware of your intake.

- Finally, eating is just one part of the equation. Exercise every day is the other part. Ideally, do an activity that makes you sweat and gets your heart beating fast for an hour a day—but even making small decisions like taking stairs instead of elevators or walking home from school instead of driving make a difference.

After you read this book, don't stop. Find out more about healthy eating. Choosemyplate.gov is a great Internet resource from the U.S. government that can be trusted to give good information; www.hsph.harvard.edu/nutritionsource is a webpage from the Harvard School of Public Health where scientists sort through all the data about food and nutrition and distill it into easy-to-understand messages. Your doctor or nurse can also help you learn more about making good decisions. You might also want to meet with a nutritionist to get more information about healthy living.

Food plays an important role in social events, informs our cultural heritage and traditions, and is an important part of our daily lives. It's not just how we fuel our bodies; it's also but how we nourish our spirit. Learn how to make good eating decisions and build healthy eating habits—and you'll have increased long-term health, both physically and psychologically.

So get started now!

1

How Does Food Affect Your Body and Mind?

Food is one of the basics of life. All human beings need to eat food to stay alive. But food does much more than that. The kinds and amounts of food people eat affect their mood, energy level, attention, and more.

Food also has a lot to do with how well young people do in school and sports. Eating the right things helps students and athletes do the best they can. Making unhealthy food choices doesn't do you any favors!

Your body needs healthy food to work correctly. The better the food you eat, the better the fuel you're putting into your body for things like school, sports, spending time with friends, and more.

Eating healthy isn't just important because adults tell you to do it. You really feel the difference when you eat right. You'll do better in school. You'll get stronger in sports. You'll feel better no matter what you're doing!

Physical Health

Food affects physical health. Your physical health is how well your body is working. When you don't eat the right kinds of food, or the right amounts, things don't feel right in your body.

Have you ever gotten a headache after eating too much sugar? Or has your digestion gone crazy after eating a huge meal? Do you feel jittery if you have too much caffeine from soda or coffee? All these cases are examples of the ways food can affect how you feel physically.

When you choose the foods your body needs, you feel much better. Everyone is different, but eating healthy food can help get rid of headaches, stomachaches, and more.

Food affects the immune system too. The immune system fights off sicknesses that invade the body. It works to keep people healthy. One of the best ways to keep the immune system strong is to feed it the right foods.

Fruits and vegetables are great at helping the immune system. The **nutrients** in fruits and vegetables work with the immune system to keep it strong. And when your immune system is strong, it can fight off colds, the flu, and any other illnesses that come your way. Being sick all the time can get in the way of doing well in school and in sports. It can even keep you from having fun with your friends. If you find yourself getting sick all the time, you should look into making better food choices.

You can see food affects you right now, in the present. You also have to think about

What Are Nutrients?

People need **nutrients** to be completely healthy. Nutrients are substances our bodies can't make, but which they need to work right. Vitamins and minerals are two examples of nutrients. Luckily, foods have nutrients, which is one reason people need to eat food.

Like vegetarians, vegans don't eat meat. Vegans also don't eat cheese, eggs, milk, fish, or any other foods that come from animals, so that means a lot of fruits and vegetables!

your future self when you eat. Healthy eating will keep you physically healthy in the future too.

Unhealthy food choices can lead to all sorts of serious diseases. Heart disease, strokes, joint and bone problems, and **diabetes** are just some of the problems people have. These health problems can get in the way of your goals for the future. It will be hard for you to be successful in college or in your career, if you have a serious illness. You may not be able to earn as much money. You may not be able to travel or play sports or enjoy the activities you like best.

Luckily, you can make the choice now to eat healthy. Then you'll have a much better chance of avoiding health problems in the future.

Moods

Food changes people's moods too. Moods are the feelings. You could be in a good mood, and feel happy and energetic. You could be in a bad mood, and feel angry, tired, and frustrated. Everyone's moods go up and down.

What's Diabetes?

Diabetes is a disease in which the body can't use sugar the way it should. Diabetes is tied to being overweight.

What Does Positive Mean?

When something is **positive**, it is good or even great.

Your mood depends on a lot of things, like how much sleep you got the night before or if your friends are being nice to you. Food is another thing that affects your moods, although you might not realize it.

A big part of feeling like you're in a good mood is energy. Imagine you have to stay after school one day, to go to a club meeting. You just want to go home, and you're in a bad mood because you're tired. You didn't eat much today because you didn't like what was being served for lunch. Chances are, though, if you ate more lunch, you wouldn't be so tired right now. Then you could enjoy the club meeting, not grumble about it.

Eating enough food is important to keep your energy levels up. In turn, that helps keep moods **positive**. Not eating enough makes you tired and cranky.

Certain things in food actually help you stay in a good mood too. Scientists think some nutrients actually keep you happy, like healthy carbohydrates and some vitamins. Eating foods with those nutrients in them gives your mood a boost.

Some Foods to Lift Your Mood

Are you wondering what to eat to feel happier? Try some of these ideas:

- Eat foods with a nutrient called folic acid. Beans and spinach both have folic acid. Scientists think folic acid might help keep people's moods positive, and even prevent depression.
- Try fish more often. Fish has nutrients called omega-3 fatty acids, which might help keep people in a good mood. Try salmon, tuna, and sardines.
- Get more vitamin D. A few foods have vitamin D in them, like eggs and cheese. Cereals, juice, and milk sometimes have vitamin D added in. People actually get most of their vitamin D from the sun, so take a walk outside to feel better!

The Right Food and the Right Amount

You can choose from a lot of different foods out there. Should you eat pizza or a salad for lunch today? Should you drink milk or soda? Healthy eating is easier with a couple of good habits.

One is choosing the right foods to eat. Choosing the right kinds of food keeps you healthy and in a good mood. Choosing too many unhealthy foods make you sick and can put you in a bad mood.

The Power of Good Habits

A habit is something you've done so many times that you keep doing it without having to think about it. For example, brushing your teeth every night before you go to bed might be a habit. You don't have to think about it—you just do it. Or a not-so-good habit might be chewing your fingernails when you feel nervous. It's something else you do without thinking.

Good habits can help you out a lot in life. They help you do things that are healthy for you every day, without giving them a thought. They make it easier to do healthy things.

We usually have to make an effort to make new habits—but once we've made a new habit, then we can stop thinking about it. Some scientists say that we need to do something for at least a couple of months before it will become a habit. That means you'll have to think about making a change in your life every day for at least two months. It won't be easy. But once you have a new habit, it will help you for the rest of your life!

The other healthy eating habit is eating the right amount of food. Eating too much or too little food can make you feel not so great. Too much food makes people uncomfortable. Have you ever stuffed yourself so much you felt like you couldn't move? Being too full isn't a very good feeling. You feel tired and **bloated**. The feeling lasts for a while.

What Does Feeling Bloated Mean?

When people say they feel **bloated**, they meant that their bodies feel puffy and swollen. They feel like they're suddenly fatter than they really are. Their clothes may fit more tightly than usual, or the rings on their fingers may be tighter.

1 Serving Looks Like . . .

GRAIN PRODUCTS

1 cup of cereal flakes = fist

1 pancake = compact disc

½ cup of cooked rice, pasta, or potato = ½ baseball

 1 slice of bread = cassette tape

1 piece of cornbread = bar of soap

1 Serving Looks Like . . .

VEGETABLES AND FRUIT

1 cup of salad greens = baseball

 1 baked potato = fist

1 med. fruit = baseball

½ cup of fresh fruit = ½ baseball

 ¼ cup of raisins = large egg

1 Serving Looks Like . . .

DAIRY AND CHEESE

 1½ oz. cheese = 4 stacked dice or 2 cheese slices

½ cup of ice cream = ½ baseball

FATS

1 tsp. margarine or spreads = 1 dice

1 Serving Looks Like . . .

MEAT AND ALTERNATIVES

3 oz. meat, fish, and poultry = deck of cards

3 oz. grilled/baked fish = checkbook

 2 Tbsp. peanut butter = ping pong ball

Knowing the serving size of the foods you eat can help you keep from eating more than you need to, which can lead to weight gain.

Over time, eating too much food causes weight gain. And too much weight gain is really unhealthy.

These good eating habits really help you out a lot in school and in sports. Of course, healthy eating won't magically solve all of your problems. Even people who eat well have bad days and get sick. The point is that healthy eating makes you feel better in general. It helps you do your best and be the best person you can be most of the time.

2

Nutrition and Learning

You might be surprised to realize that food and success at school have a lot to do with each other. Healthy food and good **nutrition** will actually help you with your schoolwork. Better eating habits can lead to better attention, a better memory, and better grades! Eating the right food won't automatically make you smarter. Food isn't the same thing as hard work in school. But food will help make it easier for you to learn.

What's Nutrition?

Nutrition is all the ways you get food. Good nutrition involves making good food choices that keep you strong and feeling good. Bad nutrition involves making food choices that make you sick or that keep your body from working at its best.

School Skills

You've been sitting at your desk for an hour already, and you're bored. You can't seem to pay attention to the teacher. You know you should be, since you're supposed to be learning. Sound familiar?

Everyone gets bored in school sometimes. For some young people, paying attention is a lot harder, though. Rather than sitting at a desk, they would rather be riding their bikes or playing on the computer.

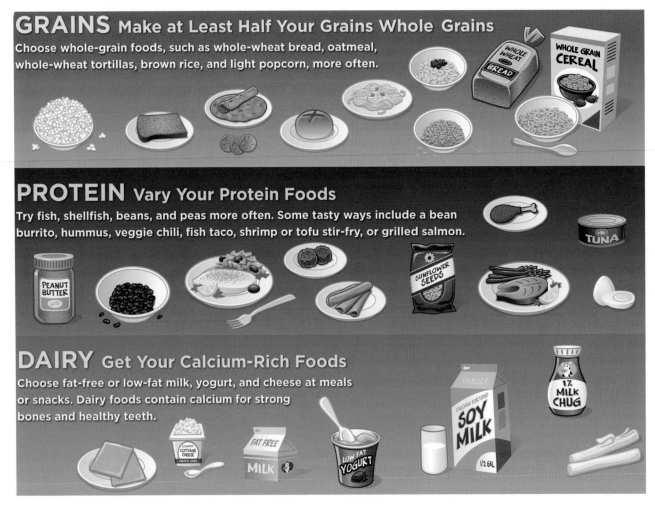

GRAINS Make at Least Half Your Grains Whole Grains

Choose whole-grain foods, such as whole-wheat bread, oatmeal, whole-wheat tortillas, brown rice, and light popcorn, more often.

PROTEIN Vary Your Protein Foods

Try fish, shellfish, beans, and peas more often. Some tasty ways include a bean burrito, hummus, veggie chili, fish taco, shrimp or tofu stir-fry, or grilled salmon.

DAIRY Get Your Calcium-Rich Foods

Choose fat-free or low-fat milk, yogurt, and cheese at meals or snacks. Dairy foods contain calcium for strong bones and healthy teeth.

Good nutrition may help you focus more in school, no matter who you are. Eating the right foods—and eating enough food—makes it easier to settle down and pay attention.

Focusing and paying attention aren't the only skills good nutrition will boost. Eating the right kinds of food also gives you energy—and that can help you learn better.

Humans eat because food is what gives their bodies energy. The energy from food keeps us going every day. We can move around because of energy. Our bodies use energy to breathe and pump blood. Energy even lets us think.

Eating the right amounts of food keeps your energy up. Skipping breakfast, for example, is bad for energy levels. You don't get the fuel you need in the morning, so you get very tired by lunchtime. Once you eat a healthy lunch, your energy shoots back up, and you'll be ready for the rest of the day—but you may not remember much from your morning classes.

Food may also help you out at school by improving your memory. Eating healthy foods keeps the brain alert. In some **scientific studies**, better food has been proven to equal better memory. You'll be able to remember all those dates for history tests and equations for math tests!

What Are Scientific Studies?

Scientists try to answer questions. They run **scientific studies** to test specific answers to specific questions. A scientist, for example, might ask whether blueberries help people remember things better. The scientist thinks the answer is yes. She designs a scientific study to test whether her answer is right or not.

Missing School

Eating well may also keep you in school more. Remember, when you eat healthy foods, you don't get sick as much, and you have more energy. You won't have to miss as much school.

Fruits like blueberries are very healthy and don't contain the sugar, fat, and salt that can leave you feeling sick and sluggish. Blueberries make a great breakfast that will give you plenty of energy for your school day.

"Brain Foods"

Some foods are just great for your brain! Eat them regularly and see if they make you learn better.

- Blueberries improve memory.
- Avocados have unsaturated fat in them, a healthy fat that keeps your brain healthy.
- Salmon has a nutrient called omega-3 fatty acid, which improves focus and memory.
- Nuts have all sorts of brain-boosting things in them. Walnuts are especially good at keeping your blood flow healthy, which in turn helps out your brain.

When you come back to school after you've been sick, you have to make up the work you missed. You might find it hard to catch up before the next test or essay. You feel like you missed out on learning some important things.

Everyone gets sick from time to time. Eating healthy won't change that. But eating healthy may keep you from getting sick so often. Your body will be able to fight off more diseases and just feel better in general.

Staying in school helps you learn better. You won't miss out on classes. You can just learn at the same pace as the rest of the class.

Better Grades

Good nutrition helps you focus and pay attention. It can improve your memory. It gives you energy to get through the whole school day. It keeps you healthy so you don't miss as many school days.

Soda and candy might give you a small boost of energy for a little while, but soon that feeling will fade. Healthier food makes better fuel for your body, giving you more energy that will last longer.

All of those great things might add up to better grades. You sit in your seat and pay attention instead of fidgeting and interrupting—so you get a better participation grade. You pay attention and remember what the teacher is saying—so you do better on tests. You don't miss an important homework assignment because you were sick—so you get a better homework grade.

Good nutrition doesn't *automatically* give you better grades. You still have to work hard! Just because you start eating better, doesn't mean you can stop doing your homework. But good food gives you a better chance of getting good grades.

> ## What Does it Mean to Crash?
>
> When you **crash** after eating something or doing something, you suddenly feel really, really tired.

The Opposite Effect

Food can make school better, but it can also do the opposite. Unhealthy eating habits can make learning even harder.

TOO MUCH SUGAR

Most people these days eat too much sugar. Unfortunately, too much sugar is really bad for health and can get in the way of learning at school.

When you eat a candy bar or drink soda, you might feel a rush of energy. All of a sudden you want to run around! Wait a little longer, though, and you'll **crash**.

The kind of energy you get from sugar isn't great for school. You want enough energy to pay attention to the teacher and not fall asleep at your desk—but instead, sugar makes you restless. That can make it even harder to pay attention. And after the effects of sugar wear off, you feel like sleeping. Sleeping at your desk isn't a good idea!

SKIPPING MEALS

Part of good nutrition is eating complete meals every day. Skipping breakfast or lunch or eating a bag of chips for dinner doesn't count as good nutrition. Although eating

What's a Chemical?

Everything in the world is made out of **chemicals**. For example, water is made out of two chemicals (hydrogen and oxygen) that join together. Foods are made from chemicals naturally. Sometimes foods have other chemicals added to them, though. Chemicals are also in medicines and drugs. Certain chemicals affect our bodies in different ways.

What Is a Sleep Schedule?

A **sleep schedule** is when you normally go to bed and when you wake up. A person who needs to sleep nine hours a night to feel good has a longer sleep schedule than a person who needs to sleep for seven hours.

at least three meals a day is important for your whole life, it's especially important for school.

Like we mentioned before, skipping breakfast makes you tired and cranky in the morning. Starting the day off hungry is not good nutrition.

The same thing goes for skipping lunch in school. Maybe you don't like what's being served, or you forgot and left your lunch at home. Or you think not eating lunch will help you lose weight. Skipping lunch doesn't make you feel good, though (or lose weight in a healthy way). Without any lunch, you'll find you're sleepy or crabby in the afternoon.

Besides being in a bad mood, you won't be learning as much in school. Learning while you're tired is really hard. You just want to relax or go to sleep, not sit at a desk and learn. Eat breakfast and lunch (and dinner when you get home), so you're ready to learn.

CAFFEINE

Caffeine is a **chemical** that speeds people up. Caffeine keeps people awake. It makes their hearts beat faster and makes it hard to sleep.

A few foods and drinks have caffeine in them. Coffee has caffeine. Soda, tea, and chocolate also have caffeine in them.

People often drink or eat caffeine to wake up in the morning, or to stay awake when they're feeling sleepy. Young people use it to feel awake at school, or to get them through after-school activities. Too much caffeine isn't good for you, though.

Caffeine gets in the way of a normal **sleep schedule**. It can make it hard to sleep at night. And the energy you get from caffeine feels good for a little while, but when it wears off, you crash and feel worse.

Caffeine is not a good way to get through the school day. A good night's sleep and good nutrition are much better ways to keep your energy up for the whole day. They'll give you the energy you need to learn—and also to have fun.

Sleep and Exercise

Good eating habits aren't the only way you can do better at school. Sleep and exercise also have a lot to do with how you feel and how well you do at school. Getting enough sleep every night keeps you awake and alert in class, not snoring. Most young people need eight or more hours of sleep every night. Exercise is also a good mood booster, just like eating healthy is. Find an exercise you like—walking, running, swimming, soccer, or anything else—and get going! Moving around makes you feel good and may even help you learn in school. Exercise also keeps you fit at a healthy weight.

3

Nutrition and Sports

After school is over, lots of young people play sports. Whether you play on a school team, in sports lessons, or at a sports club, you'll need good nutrition to do well in sports. Eating the right foods and eating enough of the right foods are important for doing your best.

Food has a lot to do with your performance in sports. Healthy food choices help you throw farther, run faster, and score more goals!

Nutrition Facts

Serving Size 1 cup (236ml)
Servings Per Container 1

Amount Per Serving

Calories 80   Calories from Fat 0

	% Daily Value*
Total Fat 0g	0%
Saturated Fat 0g	0%
Trans Fat 0g	
Cholesterol Less than 5mg	0%
Sodium 120mg	5%
Total Carbohydrate 11g	4%
Dietary Fiber 0g	0%
Sugars 11g	
Protein 9g	17%

Vitamin A 10%   •   Vitamin C 4%
Calcium 30% • Iron 0% • Vitamin D 25%

*Percent Daily Values are based on a 2,000 calorie diet. Your daily values may be higher or lower depending on your calorie needs.

Check the nutrition facts for the foods you eat online or on the package. Food labels show you the kinds of nutrients in the food you're eating, from fat and sugar to calcium and carbohydrates. You can also see how many calories are in your food.

Getting the Right Nutrients

Athletes need nutrients, just like everyone else. In fact, athletes need more of some nutrients than people who don't play sports. All the activity they do means they need to think more about their **diets** than other people might have to.

CALCIUM

Calcium keeps bones strong and keeps them from breaking. Everybody needs to eat a lot of calcium, especially young people who are still growing. Foods with calcium in them include milk, cheese, kale, and spinach.

Sports are hard on bones. Lots of athletes break bones during practice or games. Athletes who eat more calcium have stronger bones that are less likely to break.

CARBOHYDRATES

Carbohydrates are nutrients that give the body energy. Sugar is a carbohydrate. Dietary fiber and starch are two other kinds of carbohydrates.

Fiber and starch are better carbohydrates for athletes (and for anyone else). They give you long-lasting energy that will help keep you going during a game. **Whole grains**, fruits, and vegetables have long-lasting carbohydrates.

What's a Diet?

Your **diet** is everything you eat and drink. Everyone has a diet, because everyone eats. Your diet should have fruits, vegetables, grains, protein, and more.

The other kind of diet is a special way of eating to lose weight. When someone says they're "on a diet" or "dieting," he means he's trying to lose weight.

What Are Whole Grains?

Grains are the seeds of grass plants we eat. **Whole grains** are made of the entire grain seed. Whole grains have a lot of nutrients in them, like carbohydrates and protein. Examples of whole grains are brown rice, whole-wheat flour, and oats. Many grains we eat are not whole grain. They have had part of the seed taken out, so they don't have as many nutrients. Non-whole grains include white flour and white rice.

What Are Cells?

Cells are the tiniest parts of the human body. Groups of cells make up different organs, like the brain, heart, and intestines.

Sugar does give you energy, but it doesn't last for long. As soon as you use up the energy from sugar, you get really tired. Imagine losing steam halfway through a soccer game or baseball practice! Stay away from using sugar to feel energetic.

IRON

Iron helps the blood carry oxygen to **cells** throughout the body. Low iron levels make you tired because your blood can't get enough oxygen to the rest of your body. You move more slowly. A lot of people don't get enough iron. Athletes need to eat plenty of iron.

Red meat has a lot of iron. So do beans, lentils, eggs, and spinach. Even cereal and orange juice sometimes have added iron.

PROTEIN

Protein is a nutrient that builds muscles and keeps them healthy. For a lot of athletes, stronger muscles means a better game!

Eating a variety of protein sources is best. Foods like meat, eggs, beans, tofu, whole grains, and nuts have a lot of protein.

Eat protein foods after exercising to refuel. Half an hour after a long practice or a game, eat a snack with protein in it. You'll feel great and be ready to go on with your day.

Sports Snacks

You might feel hungry in the middle of playing sports. Carry some healthy snacks with you so you can refuel and keep going. Try granola bars, trail mix, whole-wheat bread and peanut butter, 100 percent juice, and fresh fruits and veggies. Snacks like these examples will give you more long-lasting energy and keep your brain active. Limit snacks like cookies and candy. They'll give you a short burst of energy and then leave you feeling tired.

Burning Up Calories

A big difference between athletes and young people who don't do sports is how much food they need. Athletes need a lot of food!

Basically, athletes need more energy than people who don't play sports. Playing sports uses up a lot of energy.

People measure the energy in food in calories. A food with more calories has more energy. A food with fewer calories has less energy.

Usually, most people need around 2,000 calories every day. Their bodies use up 2,000 calories of energy during one day. Walking uses calories. Thinking uses calories. Even just sitting and watching TV uses up calories. Add all that adds up to about 2,000 calories.

Athletes need a lot more calories. Playing sports uses up lots of calories. For example, someone playing basketball for an hour can burn over 500 calories! Two hours of playing basketball would burn 1,000 calories. And 1,000 calories is half of all the calories the body needs in a normal day. So that person might need to eat 3,000 calories in a day instead.

Even when you play sports, your body still needs energy for all the normal things it does—walking, pumping blood, breathing, thinking, and more. But athletes are using up all the energy for playing sports instead.

Athletes need more calories, so they need to eat more. More snacks are a good idea. Making meals bigger is another good idea.

Athletes have to be careful not to just eat whatever they want, though. Eating two fast-food meals every day for extra calories isn't a good choice. The food in those meals is still unhealthy and can be bad for the body. Instead, athletes should load up on more healthy foods that are nutritious and provide more calories.

Foods with protein (like meat and beans) are a good choice for athletes. They fill you up, and keep you going. Carbohydrates are also a great choice. Choose carbohydrates that will give you long-lasting energy like whole grains, not sugar.

Guzzling Water

Part of good nutrition is drinking water. People's bodies are at least half water. That means if you weigh 100 pounds, at least 50 of those pounds are water!

How Many Calories?

Different sports burn up different numbers of calories. How many calories an athlete burns depends on the sport and how long she plays the sport. People who are sitting on the bench won't be burning as many calories as the people running around on the field! How many calories someone burns is also tied to how much he weighs. People who weigh more tend to burn more calories.

Here are some examples of how many calories playing different sports burns in an hour. The numbers are based on someone who weighs 120 pounds. People who weigh less will probably burn fewer calories doing the same thing. People who weigh more may burn more calories.

Badminton: 245 calories an hour
Basketball: 463 calories an hour
Biking: 436 calories an hour
Frisbee: 164 calories an hour
Gymnastics: 218 calories an hour
Ice skating: 382 calories an hour
Soccer: 382 calories an hour
Swimming: 436 calories an hour

Our bodies need water to work right. Without water, people get sick. The way we get water into our bodies is by drinking it. Food also has water in it. Watermelon, for example, has a lot of water, but most foods have at least a little water in them.

Thirst is the way our bodies tell us we need to drink water. You should drink water *before* you feel thirsty, though, so your body is working right all the time.

Athletes need to drink even more water than people who don't play sports. Sweat is made mostly of water. When athletes sweat, they're losing a lot of water from their bodies. They need to replace it by drinking. They need to drink before playing a sport, while they're playing, and after they play. Any opportunity to drink water is a good opportunity!

Getting enough to drink is particularly important when it's hot. People sweat more and get **dehydrated** more easily in the heat. Also, the longer the sports practice or game, the more water you need to drink.

What Does Dehydrated Mean?

When someone is **dehydrated**, his body doesn't have enough water to function well.

Being active and playing sports is an important part of staying healthy as a young person. No matter what activity you choose, any kind of exercise helps you be fit and strong. But activity is only half of the health game. The other half is good nutrition. Be sure to eat right to get the most out of your sport and to be the best athlete you can be!

4

Staying Healthy, Seeing Success

You've probably noticed some common **guidelines** for eating healthy at school and for sports. In fact, *everyone* should follow these healthy eating guidelines no matter what they're doing during the day. Food affects everyone. Food helps keep our muscles strong and helps keep us in a good mood.

What Are Guidelines?

Guidelines are pieces of advice. They're advice you should follow almost all of the time. Healthy eating guidelines are advice for keeping your body and mind feeling good.

You don't have to stop eating sweets or salty snacks completely, but choosing healthier foods with less fat, sugar, and salt in them is the best way to stay healthy and in shape.

Making Healthy Eating Happen

Don't just let people tell you healthy eating is important—see for yourself! Learning about healthy eating is one thing. Actually feeling the difference healthy eating makes is even more powerful.

So try healthy eating for a little while. Start with something small, like replacing a snack bag of chips with some carrots or an apple. Or switching from white bread to whole wheat bread on your sandwiches. Or deciding to eat breakfast every single day.

Pay attention to how the changes make you feel. Does eating a little less sugar get rid of the headaches you get every afternoon? Does eating breakfast give you more energy at school? Does drinking more water at sports practice help you stay in the game?

When you see for yourself how much eating healthy foods makes you feel good, you'll want to keep going. Now healthy eating isn't something other people are telling you to do. It's something you want to do.

Give yourself time to get used to eating healthy foods. A lot of the time, people just assume they won't like a new food. They don't even bother to try it. Or they try it and don't keep an open mind. Instead of giving up on a new healthy food, keep eating it. You might have to try it a few times before you decide you like it.

For example, you might think you hate brown rice. You never eat it. Then your parents make you try it one day. You barely take a tiny taste, and immediately say you don't like it. But did you really taste it? Did you have an open mind? Try it again with an open mind. Maybe you don't really like it and you don't really hate it. Keep eating it a few more times. Order it at lunch. Ask for it at dinner. Pretty soon, you'll just get used to it. You might even start to think it's really tasty! And you'll have added a new healthy food in your diet.

Fruits and vegetables are some of the healthiest foods you can eat. Eating colorful fruits and vegetables is a great way to get many of the nutrients you need to stay healthy. Instead of a bag of chips, try an apple, orange, or banana!

Good Nutrition Guidelines

To feel your best and stay healthy, stick to these guidelines.

- Eat as many fruits and vegetables as possible. Sneak them in whenever you can—cut up fruit in your cereal or oatmeal, add veggies to your sandwich, eat fruit and veggies for snacks.
- Choose whole grains. Instead of white rice and white bread, pick brown rice and whole-wheat bread. Quinoa, oats, and barley are other examples of whole grains. They have more nutrients than non-whole grains.
- Vary your foods. Eat a variety of food every day to get as many nutrients as possible. Besides fruits, veggies, and grains, eat dairy and protein. If you're vegetarian or vegan, research good substitutes for meat and dairy.
- Limit junk foods. Junk foods don't give you many nutrients, and have unhealthy amounts of sugar and salt. You don't have to cut them out entirely, but save candy, cake, cookies, chips, soda, and other junk foods for special treats.

Success in School, Sports, and Beyond

You've seen how good nutrition can help you do better in school and sports. Good food gives you school skills like focus, a good memory, and lots of energy. Healthy eating also keeps you strong at sports.

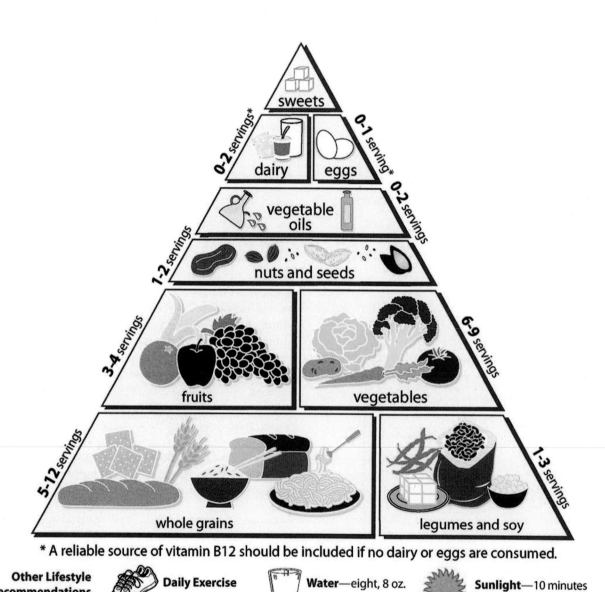

Many people get protein in their meat. Vegetarians need to make sure they get their protein from vegetables and other foods, like soybeans. Vegetarians have to eat a balanced diet like everyone else.

What Does it Mean to Be Vegetarian or Vegan?

Vegetarians choose not to eat meat. Vegans don't eat any foods that come from animals, like dairy and sometimes honey. Some vegetarians and vegans choose their diet because they don't think people should eat animals or animal products. Others decide to cut out meat or dairy for health reasons. They feel better when they don't eat meat and dairy. Vegetarians and vegans can have perfectly normal and healthy lives.

But it doesn't stop there. You have a life outside of school and sports. What about the weekend? Or the summer? Choosing to eat healthy foods is important for the rest of your life too.

Healthy eating even helps you get along better with friends. Your friends probably like to hang out with you when you're in a good mood. And you like hanging out with them when they're in good moods. The more healthy you are, the better you will get along with others.

You also want to have lots of energy when you hang out with friends. You can't agree to go play Frisbee in the park if you're feeling too tired from eating so much sugar. Eating healthy and having energy keeps you active and ready to see your friends.

Another thing healthy eating can do is give you more self-confidence. People who are self-confident think good things about themselves. People with low self-confidence think they're ugly or stupid or worthless.

A lot of young people who don't eat healthy weigh too much. Weighing too much doesn't mean people are ugly or stupid. But it does mean they might be in danger of getting sick. And lots of young people who weigh too much get teased and think they're no good. Healthy eating keeps your weight in check. Being a healthy weight and feeling good gives you self-confidence.

Eating healthy and getting plenty of exercise are the two best ways to do better in sports and school, feel better about yourself, and stay healthy as you get older.

Food helps you do better in school and on the field. When you do better, you feel better about yourself. So eating healthy can improve your self-confidence. It can make you more willing to take on new challenges. When you believe in yourself, you're more willing to try something new.

And all that comes from eating healthy foods!

Find Out More

ONLINE

Kidnetic.com
www.kidnetic.com

KidsHealth: Eating for Sports
www.kidshealth.org/kid/stay_healthy/food/sports.html#cat119

Nutrition for Kids
www.nutritionforkids.com

ProHealth- Exercise and Activity Calorie Counter
www.prohealth.com/weightloss/tools/exercise/calculator1_2.cfm

IN BOOKS

Kalnins, Saina. *YUM: Your Ultimate Manual for Good Nutrition.* Montreal, Quebec: Lobster Press, 2008.

Petrie, Kristin. *Food as Fuel: Nutrition for Athletes.* Minneapolis, Minn.: Checkerboard Library, 2011.

Simons, Rae. *I Eat When I'm Sad: Food and Feelings.* Broomall, Penn.: Mason Crest Publishing, 2009.

Index

About the Author & Consultant

Kyle A. Crockett is a freelance writer whose work can be found in print and online. His writing for young people has focused on topics ranging from health to economics.

Dr. Borus graduated from the Harvard Medical School and the Harvard School of Public Health. He completed a residency in Pediatrics and then served as Chief Resident at Floating Hospital for Children at Tufts Medical Center before completing a fellowship in Adolescent Medicine at Boston Children's Hospital. He is currently an attending physician in the Division of Adolescent and Young Adult Medicine at Boston Children's Hospital and an Instructor of Pediatrics at Harvard Medical School.

Picture Credits

Dreamstime.com:
    Wavebreakmedia Ltd: p. 8
    Monkey Business Images: p. 28, 36
    Jacek Chabraszewski: p. 18
    Twindesigner: p. 38
    Amy S. Myers: p. 44
    Yuri Arcurs: p. 22
    Plastique1: p. 24
    Brett Critchley: p. 40
    Elena Elisseeva: p. 10
    Paul Cowan: p. 12
fns.usda.gov: p. 20
Lorma Linda University: p. 42
United States Department of Agriculture: p. 16

To the best knowledge of the publisher, all other images are in the public domain. If any image has been inadvertantly uncredited or miscredited, please notify Vestal Creative Services, Vestal, New York, 13850, so that rectification can be made for future printings.